D0285733

This volume will be my last time drawing Sasuke and friends in their teen years. The thought does make me feel a little sad...but the next series will be called *Boruto: Saikyo Dash Generations*, and it will feature Boruto's generation! A much older Sasuke might appear in it too?! Look forward to it!

—Kenji Taira, 2017

SHONEN JUMP MANGA EDITION

VOLUME 3

STORY AND ART BY KENJI TAIRA

Translation: Amanda Haley
Touch-Up Art & Lettering: Snir Aharon
Design: Yukiko Whitley
Editor: Alexis Kirsch

UCHIHA SASUKE NO SHARINGAN DEN © 2014 by Masashi Kishimoto, Kenji Taira
All rights reserved.
First published in Japan in 2014 by SHUEISHA Inc., Tokyo.
English translation rights arranged by SHUEISHA Inc.

The stories, characters and incidents mentioned in
this publication are entirely fictional.

No portion of this book may be reproduced or transmitted in any form or by any means without written permission from the copyright holders.

Printed in the U.S.A.

Published by VIZ Media, LLC
P.O. Box 77010
San Francisco, CA 94107

10 9 8 7 6 5 4 3 2 1
First printing, May 2018

viz.com

shonenjump.com

NARUTO
Chibi Sasuke's
Sharingan
Legend
Volume 3
THE UCHIHA CLAN!!
Based on Naruto by Masashi Kishimoto
Story and Art by Kenji Taira

CHARACTERS
Suigetsu
Jugo
Karin
Uchiha Sasuke
TEAM TAKA

Haruno Sakura
Uzumaki Naruto
Hatake Kakashi
Kabuto
Orochimaru
Uchiha Itachi
Tobi
Konan
Pain
Kisame
Zetsu
Kakuzu
Hidan
Sasori
Deidara
THE AKATSUKI
OUR STORY
Uchiha Sasuke was once a ninja of Konohagakure Village, until he parted ways with Naruto, Sakura and the others. Now he travels as a rogue shinobi with Suigetsu, Karin and Jugo. Together, they are Team Taka. Sasuke devotes every day to the search for his big brother, Itachi. Will he ever make it to Itachi, his objective? Either way, Sasuke's long journey is bound to be eventful!

VOL. 3
THE UCHIHA CLAN!!

CONTENTS

Chapter 15: Team Taka's Big Fight!! 7
Chapter 16: Sharingan Legend All Grown-Up!! 20
Chapter 17: Beach Shack Taka 33
Chapter 18: True Tales of the Spooky Sharingan Legend 46
Chapter 19: Sharingan Legend Kids!! 58
Chapter 20: NinTuber Sasuke!! 82
Chapter 21: Sasuke vs. Suigetsu!! 107
Chapter 22: I am Jugo 126
Chapter 23: Karin's Battle!! 130
Final Chapter: The Uchiha Clan!! 135

CHAPTER 15: TEAM TAKA'S BIG FIGHT!!

UNACCEPT-ABLE!

RRRMBL
NO WAY!
LISTEN UP... I'M THE LEADER OF TEAM TAKA.
YOU'LL DO AS I SAY!!

IT'S THE PERFECT TIME TO SET THE RECORD STRAIGHT ...
THIS IS OUR FIRST BIG FIGHT...

JUGO!
I WOULD WIN A CON-TEST OF STRENGTH!

KARIN!
I'M AT LEAST STRONGER THAN SUIGETSU!

SUI-GETSU!
HMPH... I'M STRONGER THAN YOU IN THE WATER!

BA
M
TO SETTLE THE DEBATE OF WHICH ANIMAL IS THE STRONGEST IN THE WORLD!!
RRMBL
I CAN'T BELIEVE WE'RE FIGHTING OVER SOMETHING THIS DUMB...
THIS IS A HEATED BATTLE STARRING SASUKE AND HIS FRIENDS!!
TO THINK A DAY WHEN I'D FIGHT YOU GUYS WITH ALL MY MIGHT WOULD COME...

GIRAFFE

THE UCHIHA CLAN ARE ELITE GENIUSES!
DO NOT MOCK THE UCHIHA!

HE'S SERIOUSLY BECOME A GIRAFFE!!
BA
UHHHH
THERE-FORE, MY OPINION COULD NEVER BE WRONG!
M

HE WOULDN'T TAKE A DUMB DISAGREE-MENT LIKE THIS SERIOUSLY...
THAT'S RIGHT! SASUKE IS A GENIUS NINJA!

SASUKE, WHERE IS ALL THAT PASSION COMING FROM?!
...GETS A MAN'S ROMANTIC SPIRIT GOING!!
THE DEBATE OVER WHICH ANIMAL IS THE STRONGEST IN THE WORLD...
DON'T YOU GET IT, SUI-GETSU ...?

RU
MBL
HMPH... WANT TO PUT THAT TO THE TEST IN A REAL ANIMAL BATTLE, THEN?
THEY JUST PLAIN LOOK WEAK...
I'M NOT CONVINCED. I MEAN, GIRAFFES?
KRE
EEEE
I CAN'T BEAT THAT!!
AND NINJUTSU IS CHEATING!!
WITH THIS "GIRAFFE"—KIRIN!!

HIPPO

HIPPOS MIGHT LOOK GENTLE AND STUPID...
...BUT THEY'RE ACTUALLY QUICK-TEMPERED AND JUST PLAIN FAST!!

PLUS, THEIR JAWS ARE AMAZINGLY STRONG. THEIR BITE FORCE IS ONE TON!!
THEY CAN RIP ANY-BODY TO SHREDS!!
SHA

SUI-GETSU ...
YOU'RE QUITE LIKE THE HIPPO!
THE HIPPO'S HABITAT IS BY THE WATER'S EDGE...
THAT'S RIGHT. WITHOUT WATER, THEY CAN'T SURVIVE!!

!
WHOO
SH
THAT MEANS YOUR WEAK POINT IS...
ALL THE WATER IN MY BODY'S BEING SUCKED OUT BY THE CAKE...
BA
SLRRSH
GIANT DRY CASTELLA SPONGE CAKE!!
EATING CASTELLA CAKE DOES MAKE YOUR MOUTH DRY, YEAH, BUT WHAT KIND OF ATTACK IS THAT?!
M

LION

IN OTHER WORDS...
LION PRIDES HAVE MANY LIONESSES TO ONLY ONE OR TWO MALE LIONS

IT'S A KARIN LION PRIDE!!
BOOF
SHUP
BOOF
ART OF THE DOPPEL-GANGER!
BOOF

DAP
ALSO, THE LION-ESSES DO THE HUNTING!!

...THERE'S NO WAY SASUKE CAN RESIST FALLING FOR ME!!
HEE HEE HEE! WITH A HAREM LIKE THIS...

GRRWR
GYAA-AAH!!! SCARY, SCARY, SCARY, SCARY !!!
SASUKEEEE!!!
I'LL EAT YOU AAALL UP! ♡
BAM
BAM
BAM
BAM
SHISHI RENDAN! BARRAGE OF LIONS!!
GUAH!!
HE FENDED THEM OFF!!! GIRAFFES ACTUALLY ARE STRONG!!

GORILLA

THAT'S A RELIEF... SO THEY'RE GENTLE GIANTS, HUH?
GORILLAS HAVE A VIOLENT REPUTATION, BUT THEY'RE ACTUALLY QUITE MILD TEMPERED!

O-OKAY...
WELL, YOU'RE SAFE AS LONG AS YOU DON'T ANGER THEM.

WHAT THE HECK? THAT'S WAY NASTY!!
HOO!
ONLY, WHEN THEY'RE THREATENED, THEY'LL THROW POOP.

IF THAT HAPPENS, THE "STRONGEST ANIMAL DEBATE" WILL BE THE LEAST OF OUR WORRIES...
KILL!!
GA HA HA!
JUGO SNAPS OUT OF NOWHERE, THOUGH...

ZWURR
...
H...
?!
I LITERALLY JUST FINISHED THAT THOUGHT!!
UGH!
THROB
HOO HOO HOO HOO HOO HOO !!!
FLING
FLING
FLING
FLING
FLING
GYAAAAH!!! GORILLAS ARE THE STRONGEST, IN A WAY!!

THE STRONGEST ANIMAL

KABOOOM
HOW DID THINGS TURN OUT LIKE THIS?! WE WERE JUST TALKING ABOUT WHICH ANIMAL IS STRONGER!
GARGH!
THAT'S IT... I KNOW WHICH ANIMAL IS STRONGEST!
!
I DIDN'T REALIZE YOU'D GOTTEN THIS STRONG...
HUFF
HUFF
NOT BAD, YOU GUYS...
DON'T WRAP IT UP ALL NEATLY AND ACT COOL!!
THEIR STRUGGLE WILL GO ON!!
SHU
IT'S US, THE HAWK !!
F

CHAPTER 16: SHARINGAN LEGEND ALL GROWN-UP!!

THIS IS A STORY FROM SLIGHTLY FURTHER IN THE FUTURE...
HMPH...
CAFÉ
BEEN A WHILE SINCE WE'VE SEEN EACH OTHER. WE'RE ALL TOTALLY GROWN-UP NOW, AREN'T WE?
YES... SASUKE HAS GOTTEN ESPECIALLY MATURE.
FLINCH
SUGAR
AH. SASUKE, I BET YOU DRINK YOURS BLACK, RIGHT?
WE CAN EVEN APPRECIATE THE TASTE OF COFFEE NOW. VERY GROWN-UP!
THIS IS A GROWN-UP MANGA STARRING A GROWN-UP SASUKE!!
UGH... HOW CAN ANYONE STAND THIS BITTER STUFF?!
GULP
GULP
O-OBVIOUSLY! DO NOT MOCK A GROWN UCHIHA!!

LATE NIGHTS FOR GROWN-UPS

*SIGN: INN

SUIGETSU... YOU STILL HAVE A LOT OF GROWING UP TO DO.
!
WHOOPS... WHEN DID I FALL ASLEEP?
TWEET
TWEET
やど
I CAN STAY UP WAY LONGER!
YES, YES.
やど
*SIGN: INN
BA
YOU PUSHED IT TOO MUCH!! ARE YOU GROWN-UPS OR ARE YOU JUST PLAIN OLD?!
HUFF
STAYING UP THIS LATE IS NOTHING... TO A GROWN-UP...
HUFF
M

GROWN-UP SEX APPEAL

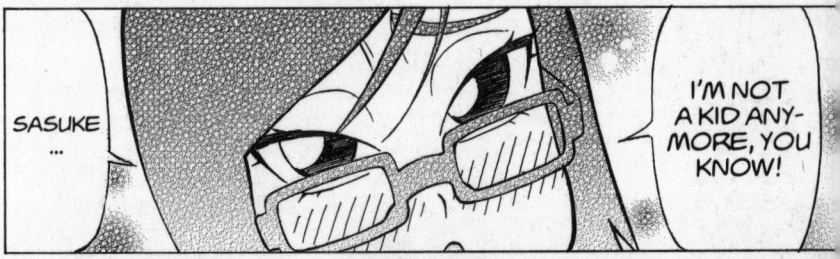

DON'T LOOK AT ME SO MUCH!!
CRACK
NOW IS THE PERFECT TIME TO USE MY EYES' NEW POWER!
RINNE SHARIN-GAN!!
GLEAM
RRRUMBL
CHIBAKU TENSEI! CATASTROPHIC PLANETARY CONSTRUC-TION!!
GYAAAAH!!! MY MAKEUP'S COMING OFF!! THE 30S WRINKLES I TRIED SO HARD TO HIDE ARE SHOWIIING!!
CRUMBLE CRUMBLE

GROWN-UP FIGHT

ODEN
ODEN
ONLY, SUI-GETSU ...
YES... HE'S GROWN, TOO...
WHOA. JUGO DIDN'T SNAP?
HE REALLY HAS GROWN UP...
YUP, HE'S A GROWN-UP ALL RIGHT!!
A WHITE-COLLAR WORKER?!
...ALL THE ANGER HE BOTTLES UP EXPLODES WHEN HE DRINKS.
THAT DIRTY BASTARD!!!
WHAM

GROWN-UP BATTLE!!

THO
PERFECT POSSES-SION FORM: SUSANO'O!!
DON'T USE SUCH POWERFUL JUTSU OVER ONE BOWL OF NATTO!!
OM
RESTAURANT
CH
OMP
TRMBL
TRMBL
IF I HAVE SUSANO'O'S PERFECT DEFENSE...

KER-
KRA
SH
GUAAARGH!!!
I JUST CAN'T HANDLE IT!!

DAD ...?
!
SKUF
HUFF
HUFF
UNGH ...
I CAME OVER HERE BECAUSE I SAW SUSANO'O, ONLY TO FIND OUT...
Y-YOU'RE ...
SARA-DA!!
BA
M
SASUKE'S DAUGHTER UCHIHA SARADA
THAT'S TOTALLY LAME.
...THAT MY DAD CAN'T EAT NATTO?
THE FINISHING BLOW?!
HANG IN THERE, PAPA SASUKE!!
SKRRR
GUAA-ARGH !!!
TOTALLY LAME?!
DON'T OVER-REACT WHEN YOU'RE OVER-SIZED!!
GAAAH

DAD ?!
BAM
SARADA. THE GIRAFFE IS THE STRONG-EST.

CHAPTER 17: BEACH SHACK TAKA!!

WHRL

WE, TEAM TAKA, FINALLY HAVE ONE...
OUR VERY OWN HIDEOUT!

IN THIS HIDEOUT, YOU WILL EACH HAVE A JOB TO DO...
UNDER-STOOD? NOW LET'S BEGIN...

THIS WILL BE OUR BASE OF OPERATIONS FOR A LITTLE WHILE...!
HEH HEH... FEELS LIKE WE'RE IN THE BIG LEAGUES NOW, DOESN'T IT?!

BA——M
WELCOME!!
UH, THIS ISN'T A HIDEOUT, IT'S A BEACH SHACK!!
UHHH
BEACH SHACK TAKA
THIS IS THE STORY OF SASUKE AND HIS FRIENDS' SUMMER!!
YOU'RE ALL GEARED UP TO HAVE FUN IN THE SUN!!
DON'T JUMP TO CONCLUSIONS, SUIGETSU... OUR OBJECTIVE HERE IS TO RAISE FUNDS FOR OUR JOURNEY!

BEACH TOYS

I HAVE A CERTAIN OBJECTIVE... AND THAT IS...
MY NAME IS UCHIHA SASUKE.

WHY ARE YOU PLAYING AROUND?! GO WORK AT YOUR BEACH SHACK!!
BOB
BOB
...TO SWIM FAR AWAY ON THIS DOLPHIN FLOATIE!

STARE
...
HUH? WHAT?

SLOOO
COME ON, ISN'T THAT A BEACH SHACK RENTAL FLOATIE?
SUI-GE-TSU ...!

I'LL TEACH HIM JUST HOW TERRIFYING I CAN BE!!
ZL
RRR
NOW HE'S DONE IT...
BA
M
HEY! I AM NOT A DOLPHIN FLOATIE!!
SPLASSHH
IT'S... A GIANT DOLPHIN !!
AWESOME!
NO, IT'S NOT!! GET A GRIP, SASUKE !!!
WOO-HOO!

PLAYBOY?

!
...HE'LL BE HITTING ON ME BEFORE HE KNOWS WHAT HIT HIM!
HEE HEE HEE... WHEN SASUKE SEES MY BIKINI...

HEY! HE'S HITTING ON ANOTHER GIRL!!
OMIGOSH! WHAT TO DO?
HOW ABOUT IT? ARE YOU FREE RIGHT NOW?
BA
M

NOW HE'S HITTING ON AN OLDER WOMAN ?!
BUH
BA
I PROMISE YOU'LL BE SATISFIED.
M

HE GOES FOR OLD GRANNIES TOO?!
BUH
BUH
BA
YOU'LL HAVE FUN!
M

OLDER MEN ARE GOOD TOO?!
BUH BUH BUH BA
I'D LOVE FOR YOU TO COME TOO, SIRS.
WHOA...
AAAUGH
M

WAIT, HE'S NOT HITTING ON ANYONE! HE'S JUST BRINGING IN CUS-TOMERS!!
BA
M
WELCOME!

LIFEGUARD

!!
SLOOO
HEEELP!!

WHOO
I'LL SPEAK WITH THE SHARK!
WAIT THERE!
SH

SPLASSSH
OH NO! A SHARK'S ABOUT TO ATTACK THAT KID!!

BUT HE CAN TALK TO ANIMALS. HE'S ACTUALLY A GENTLE GUY, DEEP DOWN...
JUGO ALWAYS SNAPS AT THE DROP OF A HAT...
U

ZL RR
... ILL...
HE'S LIKE A LIFE-GUARD KEEPING THE BEACH SAFE.
SPLASH
SPLASH
WITH JUGO ON THE CASE, THE KID'S AS GOOD AS SAVED...
RRRRU
GA HA HA HA HA!! KIIIILL!!
WAAAAH!!! SOME-THING SCARIER THAN THE SHARK'S COMING AFTER ME! HEEEELP!!!
WHAT ARE YOU DOING?! YOU WENT OUT THERE TO SAVE HIM!!
MB
LE

SUNTAN

ALL THIS TIME AT THE BEACH GAVE ME A SUNTAN!
SAME HERE.
!

I BROWNED TO A NICE TAN...
BA
UH, I DON'T THINK THAT'S A SUN-TAN!!
M

BY THE WAY, IS ACTOR MATSUZAKI SHIGERU BROWN BECAUSE ...?
THAT'S FROM A TANNING BED.
IT IS?!

UH, AND YOU HAVE WINGS ...
THIS IS FROM THE SUNTAN TOO.
WHUH?!

I MEAN, YOUR HAIR TURNED WHITE TOO...
THIS IS FROM THE SUNTAN TOO.
HUH?!

SEVERAL HOURS LATER...
I'M GOING TO TAN A LITTLE MORE...
ARE YOU JOINING ME, SUI-GETSU?
I-I THINK I'LL PASS ...
I GOT EVEN MORE TANNED!
BA
UH, YOU LOOK LIKE SOME KIND OF FINAL BOSS!!
M

SHOWER

SQUE
AK

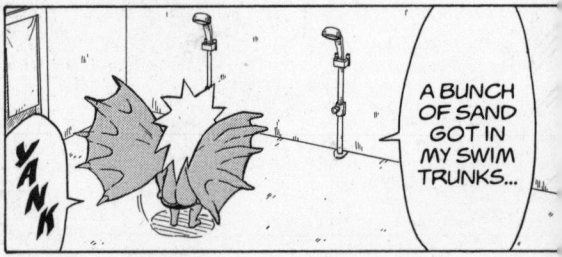
YANK
A BUNCH OF SAND GOT IN MY SWIM TRUNKS...

GUAAAH!!!
FS
S
!!!
SSHH

HUH?
URUK
OSOZAMUSO

...HURTS LIKE HECK!!
SHOOT!! TAKING A SHOWER AFTER A SUN-TANNING SESSION...

REALLY?! YOU WERE ONLY TAKING A SHOWER !!
BEACH SHACK TAKA
KABOOOM
AAAARGH!!!
IT HUUURTS!!!
HEY! OUR BEACH SHACK!!
GRRR
AND SO SASUKE AND HIS FRIENDS SET OUT ON THEIR JOURNEY ONCE MORE...
I DON'T WANNA BE FRIENDS WITH THEM!!
WELL, THE BEACH SHACK IS GONE...
...BUT WE GAINED A LOT OF FRIENDS THIS SUMMER.

CHAPTER 18:

TRUE TALES OF THE SPOOKY SHARINGAN LEGEND

ALL RIGHT...

LOOKS HAUNTED...
LET'S TEST OUR COURAGE AT THIS SHRINE.

WHAT'RE YOU SO SCARED FOR, SASUKE?
HA HA!

JOLT
A CUUURSE UPON YOUUU...
FLIK

HEH HEH ...
THIS IS A TRUE TALE OF A SPOOOOKY INCIDENT THAT HAPPENED TO SASUKE.
OKAY! I'M SORRY! YOU'RE PRETTY SCARY YOUR-SELF!
BZZZT
BZZZT
DO NOT MOOOCK THE UCHIHAAA.

SASUKE VS. THE GHOST!!

HEH HEH.. I'LL PARALYZE YOU WHERE YOU STAND...
WHAT ?!
!
SASUKE, LOOK! A GHOST!
TU
G
FINE, THEN I'LL STEP UP MY GAME ...
I CAN'T MOVE...
GLE
DO NOT MOCK THE UCHIHA. I WON'T BE OUTDONE BY A GHOST, EVEN WHEN IT COMES TO PARALYSIS!
DON'T USE YOUR NINJUTSU TO SHOW UP THE SUPER-NATURAL!!
DEMONIC ILLUSION: SHACKLE STAKES!!
AM

CHANCE FOR ROMANCE?!

THERE'S NO SUCH THING AS GHO...
RISE
HA HA! FOR CRYING OUT LOUD. KARIN'S SUCH A SCAREDY-CAT!
ZLRR
SAAASUUUKEEE...
UWAAAH!! IT'S A GHOO-OST!!!
RR
*IT'S KARIN.

ONE EXTRA PERSON...?!

WAAAH!!
WH-WH-WHO'S THIS LONG-HAIRED GUY?!
HEH HEH...
IT'S ME!
SHAKE
SHAKE
SNEER
HE'S EVEN SCARIER THAN A GHOST!!!
H...!

UCHIHA MADARA

THAT'S SUCH A STUPID WEAK-NESS!!
UGH...
WHEN I'M TINKLING AND SOMEONE STANDS BEHIND ME, MY PEE STREAM STOPS!
IT'S MY NERVOUS TEMPERA-MENT...

!
CRAP... WHAT KIND OF POWER-FUL JUTSU IS HE GONNA THROW AT US?!

WHILE I'M REVIVED, I THINK I'LL GO ON A RAMPAGE!
FOO
M
EVEN IF YOU KNOW MY WEAK-NESS, YOU STILL CAN'T DEFEAT ME!

WE'RE TAKING DOWN MADARA RIGHT HERE, RIGHT NOW!
NO, THIS IS OUR CHANCE!
WHOOSH

HUH? RIGHT NOW?!
UHHHH
AH.
EXCUSE ME...I NEED TO USE THE LITTLE BOYS' ROOM FIRST...

SHP
!!
TINKLE
GUOOOOH!!
I TOLD YOU NOT TO STAND BEHIND MEEEE!!
BLUB
BLUB
RAHHHHH!!!

I LOOK FORWARD TO MEETING YOU AGAIN...
HEH HEH... SASUKE... YOU'RE STRONGER THAN I THOUGHT...
WHY DID HE TAKE THIS MUCH DAMAGE JUST FROM SOMEBODY STANDING BEHIND HIM WHILE HE PEES?!
ZWO
UHHHH
H-HE DISAPPEARED ...
SH
UNTIL THEN ...
P
WAIT, HUH? WHERE'D MY FLASHLIGHT GO?
LET'S JUST HEAD HOME.
WHAT WAS THAT EVEN ABOUT ...?
I'LL CUUURSE YOUUU...
AFTERWARD, THERE WOULD BE STORIES OF A MYSTERIOUS GHOST SIGHTED AT THAT VERY SHRINE...
WHAT ARE YOU DOING, MADARA?!
CLICK

CHAPTER 19: SHARINGAN LEGEND KIDS!!

WELCOME TO SHINOBI KINDER-GARTEN.
BA
M
...SPEND THEIR DAYS HAVING FUN.
GOOD MORNING!
MORN-ING, KIDS!
HERE, MANY ENER-GETIC CHIL-DREN...
AND MY NAME IS UCHIHA SASUKE...

...AND IN KINDER-GARTEN!
I'M FIVE YEARS OLD...
BA
M

CALM DOWN, SUI-GETSU...
THIS CHAPTER IS A SPECIAL ISSUE.
WHY ARE WE KINDER-GARTNERS ?!

UH, SASUKE?

IS HE OUR TEACHER ...?
HMPH...
YOO-HOO! YOU TWO OVER THERE!
IT'S TIME TO GO TO THE CLASS-ROOM!

CHI-DORIII !!
NGOHHHHH!!!
CRUSH
WHAT DID YOU DO THAT FOR?!
YOU'RE A REAL LITTLE MENACE!!
THIS IS FIVE-YEAR-OLD SASUKE'S CAREFREE KINDER-GARTEN LIFE!!
LIKE I'D LISTEN TO MY TEACHER!
DO NOT MOCK A FIVE-YEAR-OLD UCHIHA!
TWITCH
TWITCH

PLAYING PRETEND

YOU GUYS REALLY ARE KIDS... THE OBVIOUS ANSWER IS...
I WILL ABIDE BY SASUKE'S WILL.
JUGO!
I WANT TO PLAY HOUSE... WITH SASUKE. TEE HEE HEE!
KARIN!
UH, WE SHOULD HAVE A PLAY FIGHT!
SUI-GETSU, YOU'RE FIRST!
BA
COME ON, PLAY SOME-THING MORE YOUR AGE!!
YOU'RE NEXT!
UGH...!
...TO PLAY REVENGE!
DUHHHHH
M
UGH ...

BSHH
WATER STYLE! DRINK-FROM-A-SQUIRT-GUN JUTSU!!
GULP
GULP

SQUEAK
SQUEAK

GLOP
GLOP

HMPH. CHILD'S PLAY...
THAT'S SO COOL, SUIGETSU! LEMME TRY!!
HEH HEH. YEAH, US WATER STYLE USERS ARE PRETTY COOL...!

PRETTY SURE DRINKING WATER FROM A MONSTER CUP IS MORE CHILDISH...
GULP
GULP
YOU STILL HAVE A LOT OF GROWING UP TO DO...
AT LEAST DRINK WATER LIKE A NORMAL PERSON.

OKAY, KIDS! IT'S NAP TIME!
SAY WHAT NOW ?!
EVEN I COULD COME UP WITH A WATER STYLE JUTSU TO RIVAL THAT.
CLICK CLICK
BA
WATER STYLE! GREAT FLOOD JUTSU!!
THAT'S JUST WETTING THE BED!!
I DRANK TOO MUCH...
M

PLAYING HOUSE

WHEN DID YOU GET A MISTRESS ?!
SHOCK
BUH BA
OH, SASUKE! WHEN ARE YOU GOING TO BREAK UP WITH THAT WOMAN, HMM?
ARE WE PLAYING HOUSE OR TRASHY SOAP OPERA ...?!
YOU AND SASUKE ARE STUCK IN A RUT! DIVORCE HIM ALREADY!
OHHH YEAH!!
WHO DO YOU THINK YOU ARE?! YOU STAY AWAY FROM MY HUSBAND!!
SHRIEK
SHRIEK

FIGHT

UH-OH! JUGO AND SUIGETSU ARE FIGHTING!!
YOU HIT ME FIRST!
DID NOT !!
BASH
CUT IT OUT!
WHAM
POW

!
YOU HIT ME ONE MORE TIME THAN I HIT YOU... THAT MEANS...
WHURR

DID TOO!
DID NOT!
HE HIT ME!
HEY! KNOCK IT OFF, YOU TWO!
WHOMP
WHOMP

HIT ME?! MORE LIKE KILL ME!!
ZWH RR
RR
...I GET TO HIT YOU ONE MORE TIME!
THEN WE'LL BE EVEN!

THERE'S ONLY ONE WAY TO STOP JUGO'S RAMPAGE ...
FINE ...
WHEN JUGO THROWS A TANTRUM, NOBODY CAN STOP HIM!!
SAVE ME, SASUKE!!
GET BACK HERE!! I'LL KILL YOU!!
HE'S EVEN MORE OFF IN HIS OWN FAIRY-TALE WORLD THAN I THOUGHT !!
I WUV ANIMALS. ♡
TEE HEE HEE
WITH THESE STUFFED ANIMALS!!

PUPPET SHOW

...AND MR. OROCHI-MARU'S PUPPET SHOW!
OKAY, BOYS AND GIRLS! IT'S TIME FOR MR. KABUTO...
BA
M

I REALLY DO NOT WANT TO WATCH THIS!
I'VE GOT A BAD FEELING...
OH BOY...

...
...

HUH... THIS SEEMS LIKE IT COULD BE FUN!
ONCE UPON A TIME, LOTS OF ANIMALS LIVED IN KONOHA FOREST.

YES, SIR!
GL O W ER
THIS PUPPET SHOW IS SCARING ME!!
DON'T SPARE THE WOMEN OR CHILDREN...
KILL THEM ALL!
BUT PEACE IN THE FOREST DIDN'T LAST...
THIS IS TOO SCARY!! IT'S GONNA MAKE KIDS CRY!!
DOO OM
AND SO, ALL OF THE ANIMALS IN THE FOREST DIED.
HAPPILY EVER AFTER.
HIC... HIC...
BOO HOOO!

CLASS KONOHA

YOU GUYS, YOU'RE KICKING UP THE DUST!
SHUP
SHUP
NEJI, I CHAL-LENGE YOU TO BATTLE!
CLEANING TIME, CLEANING TIME. ♪

THE CLASS NEXT DOOR HAS MORE PROBLEM KIDS THAN OURS...
GYA HA HA HA! AREN'T I AMAZING ?!
DUMMY
POOP
CLEAN-ING TIME...
CLEAN UUUUP !!!
STUPID
GOOD GRIEF!
CRAYONS

DUEL

SASUKE FROM CLASS TAKA AND NARUTO FROM CLASS KONOHA...
BIG NEWS!

...ARE HAVING A DUEL!

YOU'RE GOING TO LOSE TO ME HERE AGAIN...
HWOOO
THIS PLACE. I SHOULD'VE FIGURED.

TIME OUT. WHY ARE YOU ACTING ALL COOL? YOU'RE JUST STANDING ON TOP OF THE JUNGLE GYM AND THE SLIDE!!
BA M
TAMP
NARUTO-OOO!!
SASUKE-EEE!!
WHAM
THAT'S ALL?! YOU'RE COMPETING OVER WHO CAN JUMP DOWN FROM A HIGHER PLACE?!
YOU BUMBLING BUFFOON! I WAS UP HIGHER!
I WAS UP HIGHER, Y'KNOW!

PLAY FIGHT

ROAR-RR!!
SHP
RASEN-GAN!!
WHIRL WHIRL!!
SHP
SHP

THERE IT IS! THE ULTIMATE PLAY FIGHT CHEAT— THE FORCE FIELD!!
HMPH! IT DOESN'T WORK BECAUSE OF MY FORCE FIELD.
THAT'S PLAYING DIRTY!!

FORCE FIELD!
WHAP
...
KA-VOOSH !!

BZZ BZZ BZZ-ZZ !!
BZZ ...
BZZ ...
TRMBL
TRMBL
TRMBL
CHI-DORI !!

LOOKS LIKE THIS FIGHT'S A DRAW!!
HEH HEH.. I HAVE A FORCE FIELD TOO. THAT WON'T WORK ON ME!
...
...
RAHHH!
WHAP
FORCE FIELD!!
NAH! THAT'S NOT FAIRRR!!
CR
MY CHIDORI GOES THROUGH YOUR FORCE FIELD!!
USH
WHAT IS WRONG WITH YOU GUYS?!
SA-SU-KE

PLAY FIGHT PART 2

DO NOT MOCK THE UCHIHA!!
GLE
AM
HOW ABOUT YOU DON'T TURN GIANT EVERY TIME YOU GET CARRIED AWAY?!
BA
WHOOSH
UWEEN

RASENGANNN!!
CHIDORI!!!
SQUEEEZE

THE PAIR'S BATTLE TO THE DEATH CONTINUED FOR AN ENTIRE HOUR..
THAT'S TOO LONG !!
DON'T TURN GIANT JUST TO CRUSH EACH OTHER'S NADS!!!
UHHH
BAM
DOZE
DOZE
THEY'RE TRUE KINDER-GART-NERS !!
THEY TUCKERED THEM-SELVES OUT...
UGH ...!
TWITCH
YOU'VE FINALLY COME TO, EH...
...SASUKE?
BUHBAM
SHUT UP... YOU BUFFOON.
COME ON, YOU GUYS, DON'T WET THE BED!!
SASUKE'S FUN DAYS CONTINUE!!

CHAPTER 20: NINTUBER SASUKE!!

SIGH...

I'M THE ONE HOLDING THIS TEAM TOGETHER...
TRY NOT TO DRAG ME DOWN, YOU GUYS...

...
...
FORGET SASUKE, SUIGETSU IS ALL THE RAGE RIGHT NOW!
BA M
WHOAAA!! IT'S SUI-GETSU!!
CAN I SHAKE YOUR HAND?!

!
TAK
TAK
WHAT WAS THAT ABOUT?

*SIGN: INN

...

NINJA CENTERFOLD
COMPILATION
NARUTO
1,000,000 VIEWS

A READING OF MAKE-OUT
TACTICS
KAKASHI
600,000 VIEWS

NINTUBE IS...!

THESE ARE THE UPLOADED VIDEOS OF NINTUBER SASUKE!!

DO NOT MOCK THE NIN-TUBERS!

BAM

MY NAME IS NINTUBER SASUKE!

...

CARD OPENING

OPEN IT LIKE THIS!!!
SAW
SAW
NINJA-CARD
STAGGER
WHOOPS ...!
THIS WILL BE AN UNFORGETTABLE VIDEO!
KONOHA
...USING MY SHARINGAN!
SAW
SAW
HEH HEH... I ALREADY SAW THAT THESE PACKS HAVE A BUNCH OF RARE CARDS...
SHP SHP SHPSHPSHP
IN A WAY, IT DID TURN OUT TO BE AN UNFORGETTABLE VIDEO.
NO!! ALL MY RARE CAAARDS !!

VR GAME

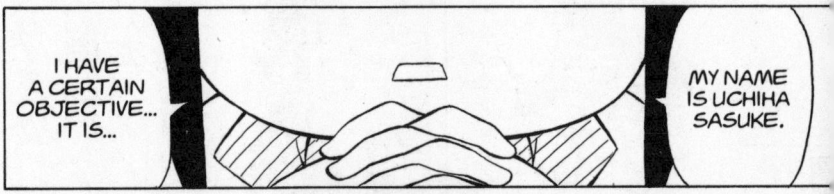
I HAVE A CERTAIN OBJECTIVE... IT IS...
MY NAME IS UCHIHA SASUKE.

BA
M
...TO PLAY THIS VR GAME!

BY WEARING A HEAD-MOUNTED DISPLAY, YOU CAN EXPERIENCE THE GAME'S WORLD AS IF YOU'VE STEPPED INTO IT YOURSELF.
GRR
!
WHAT'S A VR GAME, YOU ASK? IT'S A VIRTUAL REALITY GAME.

HEH HEH... WATCHING PEOPLE PLAY VR GAMES CRACKS ME UP!
SWING
SWING
UOHHHHH!!

SHP
SHP
SHP
SHP
HMPH... DO NOT MOCK THE UCHIHA!!

THIS SKILL TAKES A LITTLE TIME...
BZZT
BZZT
!
YOU LEAVE ME NO CHOICE ...
CHI-DORI !!
GRRR...
CRACKLE
CRACKLE
GUAAHHHH!!
CRACKLE
CRACKLE
CRACKLE
CRACKLE
CRACKLE
WHAT IS WRONG WITH YOU?! IF YOU USE CHIDORI IN ACTUAL REALITY, OF COURSE YOU'RE GONNA SHOCK YOURSELF!!
EVEN THE DAMAGE IS REAL!! SO THIS IS VIRTUAL REALITY!!

SURPRISE SHOCK

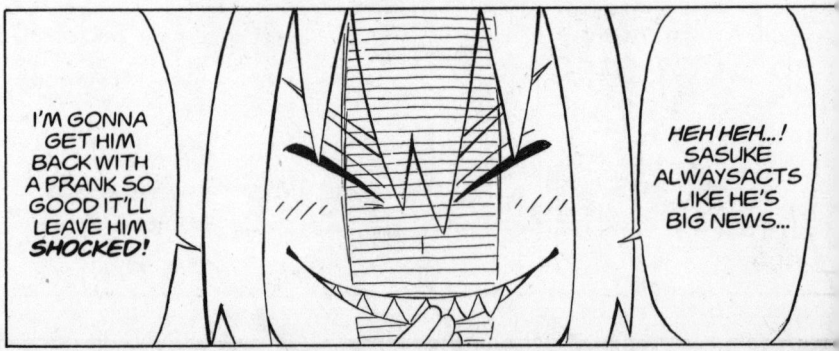

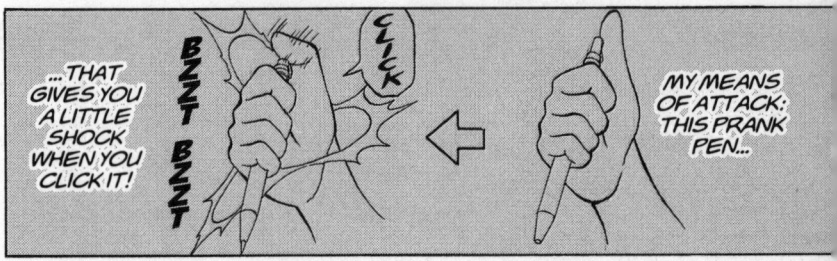

OOPS ...
SLIP
CLACK
UH, I'M PRETTY SURE THAT'S MORE THAN A SIMPLE PRANK SHOCK!!
BZZT
I'LL SHOW YOU A MORE TERRIFYING PRANK SHOCK PEN!
BZZT
CHI-DORI !!
OH, COME ON! YOU'RE JUST SHOCKING YOURSELF!!
CRACKLE
CRACKLE
CRACKLE
CRACKLE
GUAARRRGH!!
WHO PUT THIS CRAZY SHOCK PRANK HERE?!!

INTERNET IDOL

VRRR
CLACK
BA
M
KARIRIN FORGOT TO TURN OFF THE CAMERA, AND HER VIEWERS SAW HER LIKE THEY'D NEVER SEEN HER BEFORE.
VRRR
PANT
NUZZLE
PANT
NUZZLE
HEE HEE HEE HEE! SAAASU-UUKEEE!

PRODUCT REVIEW

KWEEEN
WH
AM
WHOO
SH
BOOOM
GWA HA HA HA HA!! SO MUCH FOR THE LATEST SMART-PHONE!
THIS WILL BREAK IT INTO ITTY BITS!!
JUGO, YOU'RE NOT CUT OUT TO BE A NIN-TUBER!!

SASUTARO

Tek
Tek
Tek
PPAP
Tek
Tek
Tek
Tek
Tek
Tek
Tek
Tek

I HAVE AN APPLE!
APPLE

I HAVE A PEN.
PEN

APPLE-PEN!
UH!

I HAVE A PINEAPPLE.
PINEAPPLE

I HAVE A PEN.
PEN

PINEAPPLE-PEN!
UH!

PINEAPPLE-PEN...

APPLE-PEN...

PEN-PINEAPPLE-APPLE-PEN!
UH!

LOO
LOO
LOO
TOO

ITACHI CHANNEL

ITACHI HAS A VIDEO WITH MORE VIEWS THAN YOUR VIRAL VID, SASUKE...
WHAT?! WHAT COULD IT BE...?
CLICK CLICK
WHAT IS ITACHI DOING ?!!
P.P.A.P IN SUSANO'O COMPLETE POSSESSION FORM
TEK TEK TEK
TEK TEK TEK TEK TEK
BABABAM
BABOOM
HE'S A NINTUBE MENACE !!!
DON'T DO THE P.P.A.P DANCE LIKE THAT!!
50,000,000,000 VIEWS

ANIMAL VIDEOS

GLE
AM
I'M PUTTING ALL OF YOU UNDER MY CONTROL!
LISTEN UP...
...BIJU.
A CAT TEASER?! REALLY?!
BA
M
WITH THE POWER... OF THIS!
HE'S GOING TO USE THE SHARINGAN ON THEM!
I GET IT.
BAM BAM BAM BAM
IT HAD NO POWER AT ALL !!!
NUAAAHHH !!!!

VIDEO BATTLE!!

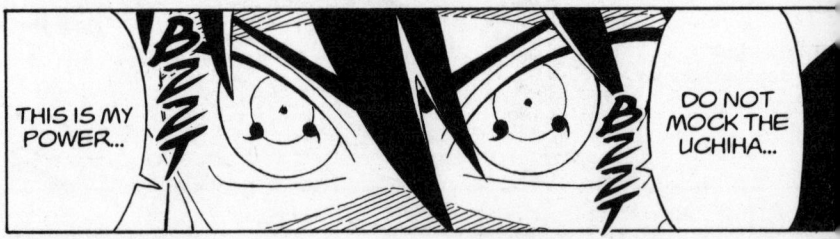

HE FIRED OFF A VIDEO!!
KREE
NEW P.P.A.P. VIDEO!!
EE
ARGH! WHAT EVEN IS THIS?!
SLO
YOGURT BATH VIDEO!!
OSH
FLA
COMPETITIVE GAME LET'S PLAY! KILLING 100 OPPONENTS VIDEO!!!
DIE!!
SH
KARIRIN OBSESSES OVER SASUKE MERCH VIDEO!!
WHOO
SH

CLU
100 PEOPLE COVER P.P.A.P. NAKED WHILE LAUGHING OBSESSIVELY VIDEO!!!
DURR
HURR
ALL OF OUR VIDEOS COMBINED INTO A SINGLE MONSTROSITY!!!
NK

WHO WOULD SUB-SCRIBE TO THIS?!
WHAT EVEN IS IT?!
HURR
DURR
IF YOU LIKED THIS VIDEO, CLICK THE "THUMBS UP" BUTTON.
IF YOU HAVEN'T SUBSCRIBED YET, PLEASE DO!
DURR HURR HURR HURR
...
DURR HURR DURR HURR
SUBSCRIBE TO CHANNEL
SHISH
NINTUBER SASUKE'S VIDEO UPLOADS WILL CONTINUE!
I SUB-SCRIBED TO YOUR CHANNEL!
CLICK
SA-SUKE...

ITACHI'S BEEN ON FIRE LATELY...
VRRR
KISAME, ROLL THE CAMERA.

CHAPTER 21: SASUKE VS. SUIGETSU!!

SLA
SH

BA
M
YOU SAVED MY BUTT, SASUKE ...
IS THAT THE LAST OF THOSE ROGUE SHINOBI?
THUHUD

SASUKE'S BEING CONDE-SCENDING AGAIN...
HMPH
DARN IT...

...YOU BIG CHICKEN?
HEH
ARE YOU OKAY...

... THEN NOBODY COULD BEAT ME, NOT EVEN SASUKE!!
IF I ONLY HAD ALL THE BLADES OF THE LEGENDARY SEVEN NINJA SWORDS-MEN...

IS THAT THE STATION'S LOST AND FOUND CORNER?!
OX STATION
LOST & FOUND
!
WHERE COULD THE OTHERS BE?
SHIP
BUT THIS IS THE ONLY SWORD I HAVE...
HOW DID THEY ALL END UP IN THE LOST AND FOUND ?!!!
LOST & FOUND
BA
M
THNK THNK THNK THNK THNK
!
SHUF
HEY. WHERE DID SUIGETSU GO?

ZAM
I'M INVINCIBLE NOW!
I FINALLY GOT MY HANDS ON ALL OF THE SEVEN NINJA SWORDSMEN'S SWORDS!

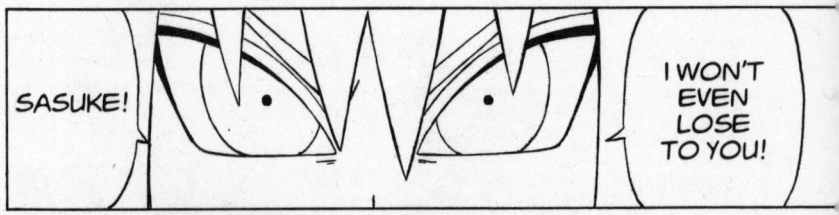
SASUKE!
I WON'T EVEN LOSE TO YOU!

RUMBLE
GET TO THE POINT, SUI-GETSU.
YOU ALWAYS ACT LIKE YOU'RE BETTER THAN ME...

HAVE IT YOUR WAY, SUI-GETSU ...
I'LL PROVE THAT I'M STRONGER THAN YOU!!
FIGHT ME, SASUKE!
BA
HEY, DON'T USE MY LEGENDARY NINJA SWORDS TO PLAY POP-UP PIRATE!!
I'LL GO FIRST!!
THNK
THIS IS THE STORY OF A HEATED BATTLE STARRING SUIGETSU.
M

THE LIGHTNING BLADE, KIBA THE FANG

ACK!
SLIP
YOUR LIGHTNING WON'T WORK ON ME NOW, SASUKEEE!!
BZZT
BZZT
AN EYE FOR AN EYE, A TOOTH FOR A TOOTH... LIGHTNING FOR LIGHTNING!
BOO
SH
YOUR OWN LIGHTNING ATTACK WORKS ON YOU!!
BZZT
BZZT
BZZT
BZZT
GUAAARRRGH!!

SAMEHADA

IT SHAVES!!
BA
GREAT BLADE SAMEHADA, THE SHARK SKIN, DOESN'T SLICE...
SKREE...
M

SHAVE
I KNOW THAT SWORD...
I WON'T LET YOU SHAVE AWAY MY CHAKRA SO EASILY...

CA
CLANG

SHAVE
SHAVE
SHAVE
SHAVE
GREE!
LUNGE
WHOA! IT'S MOVING ON ITS OWN!
WHERE IS THIS SWORD SHAVING ?!!
WHAAAT ?!!
GRIN
TEAM TAKA? FORGET HAWKS, WE'RE MORE LIKE BALD VULTURES NOW!!
DUHHH
BA
SUIGETSU... THAT'S ENOUGH PLAYING AROUND...
HEHEH
TEAM TAKA HAS AN OBJECTIVE!
HEHEH
M

HIRAMEKAREI, THE FLATFISH

SHUP
SHUP
SHUP
WATER.
GINGER!!
SAKE.
MIRIN.
SOY SAUCE.
NICE TRY!
FOOM
BA
STEWED FLATFISH!!
YOU LITERALLY COOKED IT?!
M

SO MANY SWORDS

THE LONG SWORD, NUI-BARI!!
SHP
SHP
SHP
SHP
SHP
WHA
THE BLUNT BLADE, KABU-TOWARI!!
KABOOM
HE'S GOT A GREAT HANDLE ON ALL OF THE DIFFERENT BLADES!!
AND HE'S ALSO GOT ONE MESSED-UP PERSON-ALITY!!
BLOW UP, LIFE HAVERS !!!
THE EX-PLOSIVE SWORD, SHIBUKI!!

BIG BROTHER

YOUR CLAN ISN'T THE ONLY ONE WITH INCREDIBLE MEMBERS OUT THERE!
SASUKE ...

...WAS ONE OF THE SEVEN NINJA SWORDSMEN AND COULD HANDLE ALL SEVEN BLADES ...
HE WAS EVEN CALLED THE SECOND COMING OF THE DEMON!!
MY BIG BROTHER, HOZUKI MANGE-TSU...

HOW DID THIS TURN INTO A STORY ABOUT YOUR BIG BROTHER BEATING YOU IN A FIGHTING GAME?!
HUH?! YOU'RE USING RANDOM SELECT AGAIN ?!
SHOCK
HEH!
HE WAS SO STRONG ...
...THAT HE COULD EVEN KICK BUTT AS ANY CHARACTER IN NARUTO: ULTIMATE NINJA STORM!!

IN FACT...
MY BIG BROTHER WIPED OUT OUR ENTIRE CLAN...
HMPH.. YOU AREN'T THE ONLY ONE WITH A STRONG BIG BROTHER...

ARE ALL LITTLE BROTHERS DESTINED TO GET BEATEN IN FIGHTING GAMES?!
SHOCK
SASUKEEE!
HE EVEN WIPED OUT ALL OF MY MAIN CHARACTERS IN NARUTO: ULTIMATE NINJA STORM!!

WHAT IS WITH THIS STUPID BIG BROTHER-BAD-MOUTHING CONTEST?!
ITACHI WAS ALWAYS SAYING "SORRY, SASUKE" ...
MY BIG BRO SENDS ME OUT TO BUY JUMP FOR HIM!
MY BIG BRO CHEATS AT HIDE-AND-SEEK!
YEAH, WELL MY BIG BRO EATS MY YOGURT!

CLASH!!

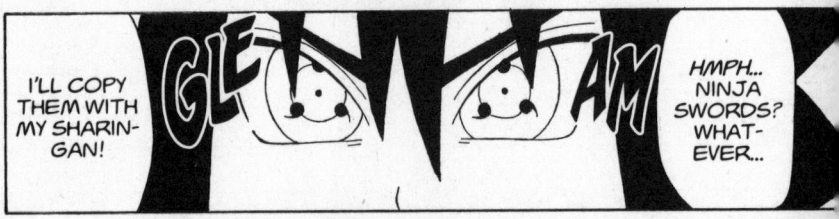
I'LL COPY THEM WITH MY SHARIN-GAN!
GLEAM
HMPH... NINJA SWORDS? WHAT-EVER...

COPY THEM?! YOU JUST MADE THEM ALL OUT OF CARD-BOARD!!
BA
DO NOT MOCK THE UCHIHA!
ORANGE?
amazon
M

BECAUSE YOU GOT SOME CARDBOARD SWORDS?!
I'M THE STRONGEST IN THE WORLD NOW...
ORANGES

AS LONG AS YOU HAVE LIGHTNING STYLE, I'D BE HARD-PRESSED TO WIN...
BUT I'M A DIFFERENT MAN NOW!
HMPH ...
DO NOT MOCK THE...
YOU ALWAYS TALK ALL HAUGHTY LIKE THAT...
BZZZT
BZZZT
I WOULDN'T EVEN LOSE TO OROCHI-MARU...
...OR TO YOU!!
AS I AM NOW...
PA
FF
SLRRR
DO NOT MOCK...
...THE HOZUKI CLAAAN !!!

SLOOSH
WATER STYLE: SEVEN NINJA SWORDSMEN WATER DOPPEL-GANGERS!!!
BZZZT
I'LL CANCEL OUT YOUR LIGHTNING STYLE WITH THIS SWORD!
DROP
ACK !!
BZZZT BZZZT BZZZT BZZZT
GUAAARGH!!!

KIRIN !!!
KREEEEEE
YOU JUST DEFEATED YOURSELF!!
HE MADE UP WITH SASUKE.
LEAVE IT TO SASUKE TO DEFEAT ME... YOU REALLY ARE A GENIUS...
...
SIZZ

CHAPTER 22:
I AM JUGO

AND I HAVE A CERTAIN OBJECTIVE...
MY NAME IS JUGO...
...THE WAY OF LIFE OF THIS MAN... UCHIHA SASUKE!!
TO ASCERTAIN...
DID HE DISCOVER AN ENEMY WHO WAS HIDING SOME-WHERE?!
!
THAT'S SASUKE FOR YOU...
SHU
P
!

WHACK
WHACK

HYAH!
SPIN

...
CAN'T REACH THE REMOTE ...
RATS !!

...

SHATTER
WHIRL
WHIRL

TO THINK HE'D NOTICED ME TOO...
THAT'S SASUKE FOR YOU...
!!
GLEAM
JUGO...
I KNOW YOU'RE THERE...
A RERUN OF PARTNERS IS ABOUT TO START. GRAB ME THE REMOTE...
WHAT THE HECK HAVE YOU GUYS BEEN DOING IN HERE?!
GROOOSH
I WILL ABIDE BY SASUKE'S WILL!
HE TRULY IS NO ORDINARY MAN...

CHAPTER 23: KARIN'S BATTLE!!

SH
P

WILL I MAKE IT IN TIME?!
TAP
TAP
TAP
THERE'S NO MISTAKE! IT'S UP AHEAD!

SASUKE'S NAKED BODY IS WAITING FOR ME BEYOND THESE FLAPS!!
HEE HEE HEE HEEEEE!!
OOH LA LA

BATHS
MEN
SHUF

C...COULD THEY BE SASUKE'S FRESHLY STRIPPED GARMENTS?!
I TH-TH-THOSE CLOTHES!!

SHUF
!!

PANT
PANT
HEE HEE HEE! OH, SASUKE-EEE!
KARIN? WHAT ARE YOU DOING WITH MY CLOTHES?!
DON'T MISLEAD ME LIKE THAT!!!
POW
GYAAAH !!!
YOU WON'T GET AWAY FROM ME THIS TIME, SASUKE-EE!!
THERE HE IS!
ZRR
MY TRUE TARGET IS SASUKE'S NAKED BODY!!
SHUP
ENOUGH OF THAT ...
PANT
PANT
WHY ...?

GWSH
GOODNESS, WHAT'S THE BIG IDEA...?
BA
M
WHY THE HECK IS OROCHI-MARU IN HERE?!
GYAAAAH!
POW
I SAW OROCHI-MARU'S BIG SNAKE!!!
HUH?
FLUTTER
ALL RIGHT... GUESS I OUGHT TO GET IN NOW TOO...
SWISH
!
BA
M
WHAT HAPPENED HERE?!
KARIN'S LOVE STORY CONTINUES...

STATION
THE HIRAME, KARE!...
THE SAME-HADA...
HUH? YOU SAY YOU LOST YOUR SWORDS?

FINAL CHAPTER:
THE UCHIHA CLAN!!

FWO
O O.O

WHAT I'M SEEING RIGHT NOW, ITACHI...
...IS YOU DEAD AT MY FEET.

THOSE SHARIN-GAN...
HOW MUCH CAN YOU ACTUALLY SEE?
FOX

THIS IS IT! SASUKE AND ITACHI'S BIG FACE-OFF!
SHUFFLE
...IN A SHARINGAN VS. SHARINGAN SHOWDOWN!! WHO'S GONNA WIN...?!
TWO NINJA GENIUSES... THE TWO SURVIVING MEMBERS OF THE UCHIHA CLAN...
ARE THEY BOTH SEEING THROUGH EACH OTHER'S ATTACKS?!
SO, THIS IS WHAT A BATTLE BETWEEN SHARINGAN USERS IS LIKE!!
!
!!
THAK
THAK
THAK

IS THIS A LITERAL SHARIN-GAN SHOW-DOWN?!
THAK
THAK
THAK
THAK
THAK
THAK
SHARINGAN
BONK!!
I'VE SURVIVED THIS LONG FOR THE SOLE PURPOSE...
ITACHI... YOU WIPED OUT THE UCHIHA.
BA
M
YOUR EYES AREN'T BACK IN!! YOUR EYES AREN'T BACK IN!!
...OF KILLING YOU!!

PUSH
HUH?
SUIGETSU, PRESS THE BUTTON ON MY BACK!
HUH? FOR REAL?! WHAT DO WE DO?!
WHAT'S WRONG WITH YOU?! YOU GUYS ARE REALLY JUST IDIOTS, AREN'T YOU?!
OW, OW, OW, OW! THEY WON'T GO BACK IN!
WOBB~LE
WHY ARE THEY GOING BACK IN LIKE A VACUUM MACHINE CORD?!
SNAP
THIS IS A GAG MANGA STARRING THE UCHIHA CLAN!!

TAIJUTSU BATTLE?!

A-RIDING ON A POO-ONY!
STUCK A FEATHER IN HIS CAP!
AND CALLED IT MACA-ROOONI!
SHP
SHP
SHP
SHP
SHP
YAN-KEE DOO-DLE ...
WENT TO TOWN!
CLAP
LAAA, LA, LA, LA! LA LA LA! LAAA, LA, LA, LA, LAAA, LA! LAAA, LA, LA, LA, LA LA LA! LA, LA, LA, LA, LA, LAAA LAAA!
I THOUGHT THIS WAS A BATTLE! THEY WERE JUST DOING "YANKEE DOODLE" AT LIGHTNING SPEED?!
DUHHH
SHP
SHP
SHP
SHP

SORRY, SASUKE

WAVE
WAVE
WHY DID YOU EAT MY CHIPS?!
YOU JUST DESTROYED IT!!
WHERE'S YOUR EVIDENCE?
WH... WHAAAT?
CLASP
I CAUGHT YOU LITERALLY RED-HANDED!!
SORRY, SASUKE...

SUPERHEROES

ITACHI MAN GIRL!
BA-M
UHHH
HUH? WHY ARE YOU A GIRL?!
YOU LOOK LIKE YOU'RE GONNA GET ARRESTED FOR A CRIME, NOT FIGHT IT!!
WAIT A SEC, ISN'T THAT MOM'S CLEAN LAUNDRY?
HEH HEH HEH ...
STOMP
US TWO CAN BEAT ANYTHING NOW! EVEN A GIANT MONSTER!
ROAR
ITACHI... SASUKE... JUST WHAT DO YOU THINK YOU'RE DOING?!
IT'S NO USE! WE CAN'T BEAT THIS FOE!!!
MOM!!
QUIVER
QUAKE

BATHTIME

YES, MOM!
GO GET IN THE BATH WITH YOUR FATHER.
ITACHIII. SASU-KEEE.
BA
M
BUBBLE
BUBBLE
THAT'S MY BOY.
ITACHI ...
BA
M
SPLSH
WHEW. I THINK I'M READY TO GET OUT...
GLE
AM
SPLASH

GAAAH
SASU-KE...
FOLLOW YOUR BIG BROTHER'S EXAMPLE AND MAKE ME PROUD.
I'M GONNA GET OUT TOO!
GLEAM
SPLASH
BA
THAT'S OUR DAD!!!
DO NOT MOCK THE UCHIHA!
ALL RIGHT... I'M DONE HERE TOO...
WHIRL
SPLASH

THAT DAY
HWOOO
I PRETENDED TO BE THE KIND OF BROTHER YOU HOPED FOR...
...TO DETERMINE YOUR ABILITY.
IT'S NOT TRUE...
MY BROTHER WOULDN'T DO THIS.
HUFF
HUFF
BECAUSE ...
FOOLISH BABY BROTHER...
AS YOU ARE NOW, YOU'RE NOT EVEN WORTH KILLING.

WHY ARE YOU GETTING SO SERIOUS OVER A GAME OF OTHELLO WITH YOUR LITTLE BROTHER?!
THE WHOLE BOARD'S BLACK!!
...THEN RESENT ME! HATE ME!
GAAAH
BA
IF YOU WISH TO KILL ME...
M
...
BAM
I'M NOT HERE TO GET REVENGE OVER OTHELLO!!
ALL RIGHT. THIS TIME, I'LL LET YOU GO FIRST...

THE UCHIHA CLAN

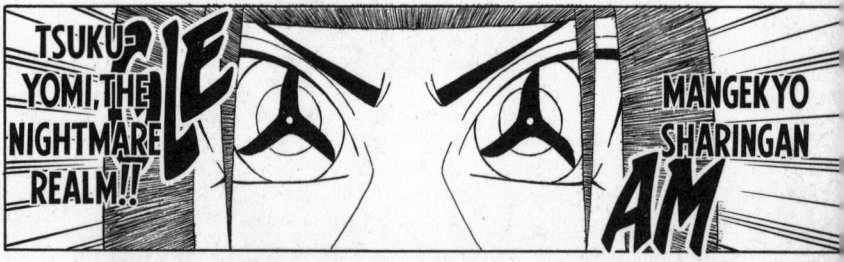

RROM
GENJUTSU! REVIVAL OF THE UCHIHA CLAN!!
GLE
AM
THIS IS BAD!!
IT'S SUCH A POWERFUL ILLUSION!

MANGEKYO
SHARINGAN
BONK!!!
MB
LE
R
RU
MB
LE

THAT'S NO WAY TO ATTACK WITH YOUR ULTIMATE EYES!!!
RU
R
POKE
POKE
POKE
POKE
CHI-DORI !!
GUARRRGH!!
WHRL
WHRL
...
AHHHH!!
T
SS
!
THE ILLUSION LIFTED!
YOU'VE GOTTEN STRONGER, SASUKE...
HUFF
HUFF
NO, YOU'RE JUST STUPID !!

THIS IS IT

BA
M
HUFF
HUFF

IS THIS... THE DEATH SCENE...YOU WANTED TO CREATE?

THUD
IT'S FINALLY OVER...

IT'S OVER...
U

CRUNCH
CRUNCH
CRUNCH
CHIPS
TOMATO BASIL
!!

...THE TOMATO AND BASIL CHIPS I WAS SAVING FOR LATER...?
HUH? AREN'T THOSE...

HEY! YOU DON'T HAVE TO EAT EVEN THE CRUMBS AT THE BOTTOM OF THE BAG!!
...THIS IS IT.
SHFF
CHIPS
SORRY, SASUKE...

OF COURSE IT HAD TO BE SOME CHILDISH FIGHT!!
AND SO, THE UCHIHA BROTHERS' LONG BATTLE FINALLY CAME TO AN END!
I'LL GONNA KILL YOU FOR THIS!!
YOU BIG JERK !!
TAP
TAP
CHIPS
THORRY, THATHUKE. (SORRY, SASUKE.)

THE END OF THE JOURNEY...?!

...TO DESTROY KONOHA!
RAHHH!!
THERE'S SOMETHING I'VE BEEN THINKING FOR THIS WHOLE JOURNEY... YOU JUST WANT TO PLAY AROUND, DON'T YOU?!
YOU MEANT DESTROY THEM IN A VIDEO GAME?!
SASUKE'S DAYS OF FUN CONTINUE!!

BONUS MATERIAL MINI MANGA CHAPTERS

MINI MANGA 1: LET'S GO TO THE NARUTO ART EXHIBIT! (ROCK LEE VERSION)

(from *Saikyo Jump* 2015 No. 3)

MINI MANGA 2: LET'S GO TO THE NARUTO ART EXHIBIT! PART 2 (ROCK LEE VERSION)

(from *Saikyo Jump* 2015 No. 5)

A Rock Lee version of the *Naruto Art Exhibit* manga. The content is pretty similar to the Sasuke version that was included in the previous volumes, but since we did it, we included this version for your enjoyment, too.

MINI MANGA 3: ROCK LEE'S YOUTH AT FULL POWER COOKING PART 1: FRENCH TRAINING ARC

MINI MANGA 4: ROCK LEE'S YOUTH AT FULL POWER COOKING PART 2: NARUTO VS. NEJI ARC

I drew these for a collaboration with the gourmet guide website *GURUNAVI.*

MINI MANGA 5: SASUKE VS. THE FOREIGNER!!

MINI MANGA 6: SASUKE VS. THE DENTIST!!

MINI MANGA 7: SASUKE VS. THECOLORED TILES!!

More of Sasuke's ridiculous battles! Personally, I had a ton of fun drawing these silly Sasuke Vs. XXX battles!

(from *Jump Victory Carnival Official Guidebook 2016*)

MINI MANGA 1: LET'S GO TO THE NARUTO ART EXHIBIT! (ROCK LEE VERSION)

*IN TOKYO FROM APRIL 25-JUNE 28, 2015, AT THE MORI ARTS CENTER GALLERY (ROPPONGI HILLS MORI TOWER FLOOR 52)

*IN OSAKA FROM JULY 18-SEPTEMBER 27, 2015, AT THE OSAKA CULTURARIUM AT TEMPOZAN (NEXT TO THE OSAKA AQUARIUM)

*WANT TO KNOW MORE? CHECK OUT THE OFFICIAL JAPANESE WEBSITE FOR THE NARUTO ART EXHIBIT! HTTP://NARUTO-TEN.COM

*YOU CAN PURCHASE TICKETS FROM LOPPI KIOSKS INSIDE MINI STOP LOCATIONS TOO.

GLEAM
OUT OF THE WAY, TENTEN !!
! NEJI!
GLOWER
ARE YOU GUYS REALLY ARE AN EVIL ORGANI-ZATION?!
I'M TRYING TO PURCHASE TICKETS FOR THE NARUTO ART EXHIBIT, BUT I DON'T KNOW HOW TO USE A LOPPI KIOSK...
HMPH ...
WHAT ARE YOU DOING HERE ?!
SHUF
I THOUGHT YOU WERE GOING TO ATTACK, BUT YOU'RE JUST SHOWING THEM HOW TO USE THE LOPPI MACHINE?!
1. On the top screen, press "I have a code"!
2. Enter the "33333" in the L Code field.
3. Choose your ticket type! Select "premium advance ticket," and then choose the quantity!
4. Double-check that everything on the screen is correct!
5. Take the receipt that the Loppi kiosk prints out, and take it to the register within thirty minutes to pay and receive your ticket!
BEEP
BEEP
8 TRI-GRAMS, 64 TOUCHES !!!
BEEP
BEEP
**ACCEPTED PAYMENT METHODS ARE CASH OR CREDIT CARD.
*YOU CAN ALSO BUY TICKETS ON THE WEB. FOR MORE INFORMATION, GO TO HTTP://L-TIKE.COM/NARUTO-TEN/.
*IF YOU HAVE QUESTIONS ABOUT USING THE LOPPI KIOSK, CALL THE NUMBER ON THE KIOSK TO REACH THE LOPPI CUSTOMER SERVICE CENTER.
!
RUSTLE
NOW ALL THAT'S LEFT IS TO TAKE THE RECEIPT PRINTED OUT FROM THIS LOPPI MACHINE, AND...
WEEN
ALL RIGHT. I'VE DOUBLE-CHECKED THE TICKET INFO!

YOU DON'T NEED TO GO FULL POWER! JUST BUY IT LIKE A NORMAL PERSON!!
FO
AS LONG AS YOU PAY AT THE REGISTER WITHIN 30 MINUTES, YOU CAN RECEIVE YOUR TICKET, YES...?!
OM

GFFAH!!
KA
MASTER GUY, THAT'S WAY OVER-BOARD!!
YOU FOO-OOL!!
POW
NIGHT GUY!!

JUST A NUISANCE. THROW IT AWAY!
THERE'S A COUPON OR SOMETHING ATTACHED TO THE TICKETS!

BUT YOU CAN GET *SCROLL OF WIND* INSIDE THE EXHIBIT HALL WITHOUT A VOUCHER, YES?!
YOU GUYS ARE ALL GOING TOO FULL POWER!!
ROARR
WITHOUT THAT PREMIUM VOUCHER, YOU CAN'T GET YOUR COPY OF THE EXCLUSIVE *SCROLL OF THUNDER* BOOKLET! DON'T FORGET TO BRING YOUR VOUCHER WITH YOU TO THE *NARUTO ART EXHIBIT*!!
*REMOVING THE TICKET STUB WILL INVALIDATE IT. TICKETS CANNOT BE REISSUED.

Tickets on sale at Loppi kiosks inside Lawson and Mini Stop locations nationwide, or on the web at http://l-tike.com/naruto-ten/! Use the L Code "33333"!

Sales Period for Tokyo	2/7 through 4/24		4/25 through 6/28
Ticket Type	Premium Advance Tickets	Regular Advance Tickets	At the door
Adults	¥1900	¥1800	¥2000
Middle/High Schoolers	¥1400	¥1300	¥1500
Children over 4	¥600	¥500	¥800

*Dates for the sales period of tickets for the Osaka location will be announced on the *Naruto Art Exhibit* website at a later date.

Caution:
*Taxes included in the price.
*This L Code applies only to the Tokyo location.
*Advance tickets sold only through Lawson Tickets.
*Please be advised that advance tickets are issued only at Loppi kiosks, and will not be delivered.
*At-the-door tickets are also available at the Mori Arts Center Gallery ticket counter.
*Premium booklet not for sale.
*Both the Tokyo and Osaka locations will offer the same premium booklet.
*Booklet design and contents subject to change.
*To receive your premium booklet, please present your voucher at the exhibit location during the duration of the Tokyo exhibit.
*Depending on crowding, there may be a wait time, or you may be unable to enter.

The *Naruto Art Exhibit* brings even Pain to tears!

See you at the super-deluxe exhibit!!

THE END

WHAT A BOTHER...
PA-PAAA !!
MY SOO-DON!

MINI MANGA 2: LET'S GO TO THE NARUTO ART EXHIBIT! PART 2 (ROCK LEE VERSION)

*THE NARUTO ART EXHIBIT TOKYO LOCATION IS OPEN FROM APRIL 25 THROUGH JUNE 28, 2015 IN THE MORI ARTS CENTER GALLERY (ROPPONGI HILLS MORI TOWER FLOOR 25).

THE OSAKA LOCATION IS OPEN FROM JULY 18 THROUGH SEPTEMBER 27, 2015 AT THE OSAKA CULTURARIUM AT TEMPOZAN (NEXT TO THE OSAKA AQUARIUM).

*ADVANCE TICKETS FOR THE TOKYO LOCATION ON SALE THROUGH APRIL 24, 2015. FOR MORE INFORMATION, VISIT THE OFFICIAL WEBSITE.

YES, MASTER GUY!
HE PULLED OUT A SMART-PHONE!!
BA
M
NARUTO ART EXHIBIT NOW
CHECK THE OFFICIAL WEBSITE AHEAD OF TIME TO SEE HOW CROWDED IT WILL BE!

...THEY'LL DISTRIBUTE NUMBERED TICKETS!!
CROWDS ARE EXPECTED ON SATURDAYS AND HOLIDAYS, IF NECESSARY...

DAT
THERE'S ANOTHER WAY TOO!
WHAT ?!

THEN, YOU CAN COME BACK LATER AT THE TIME SPECIFIED ON YOUR NUMBERED TICKET!!
WHAT'S WITH THAT TICKET DISTRIBUTION METHOD?!
WHUP
NUMBERED TICKET
YOU CAN GET NUMBERED TICKETS AT THE MUSEUM CONE!

GLE
BYAKUGAN!!
AM

HEY, WANT TO WANDER AROUND TOWN?
...
NOW WE'VE SECURED ENTRY INTO THE EXHIBIT!
BUT WHAT SHALL WE DO UNTIL IT'S TIME?

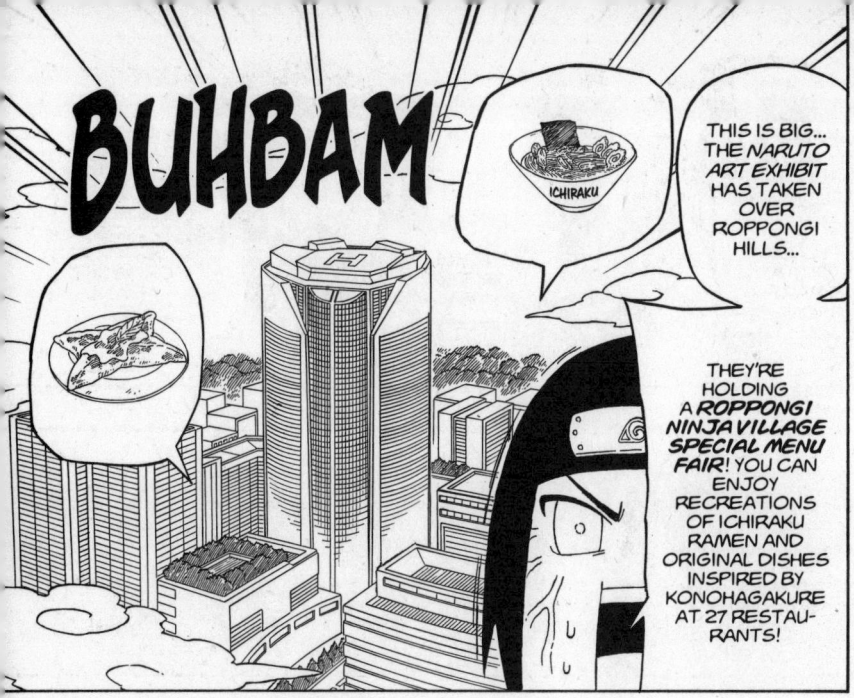
BUHBAM
ICHIRAKU
THIS IS BIG... THE NARUTO ART EXHIBIT HAS TAKEN OVER ROPPONGI HILLS...
THEY'RE HOLDING A ROPPONGI NINJA VILLAGE SPECIAL MENU FAIR! YOU CAN ENJOY RECREATIONS OF ICHIRAKU RAMEN AND ORIGINAL DISHES INSPIRED BY KONOHAGAKURE AT 27 RESTAURANTS!

DON'T SAY THAT LIKE YOU'RE USING BYAKUGAN!!
SMARTPHONE CAMERA!!
SN
AP

AND THERE'S STILL MORE TO THE FAIR...!
SLURP
IT'S DELICIOUS!

IT'S ABOUT TO START!
TO THE GALLERY!
CHATTER CHATTER
WHOOSH

THAT MEANS I CAN TAKE A FANTASY ROPPONGI DATE PHOTO WITH SAKURA!!
THAT'S JUST SAD!!
THERE ARE A WHOPPING 29 DIFFERENT CHARACTER PHOTOSPOTS SCATTERED AROUND ROPPONGI HILLS WHERE YOU CAN TAKE PHOTOS TO REMEMBER THE FAIR BY!

*PLEASE REMAIN ON THE TOUR ROUTE AT ALL TIMES.
*INSIDE THE EXHIBIT, PLEASE FOLLOW THE STAFF'S INSTRUCTIONS. FOR DETAILED GUIDELINES, SEE THE OFFICIAL EXHIBIT WEBSITE.

*SCROLL OF WIND BOOKLETS LIMITED TO ONE PER PERSON PER VISIT.
*TO GET YOUR PREMIUM SCROLL OF THUNDER BOOKLET, PLEASE EXCHANGE THE VOUCHER THAT COMES WITH THE PREMIUM ADVANCE TICKET FOR IT DURING YOUR VISIT TO THE EXHIBIT.

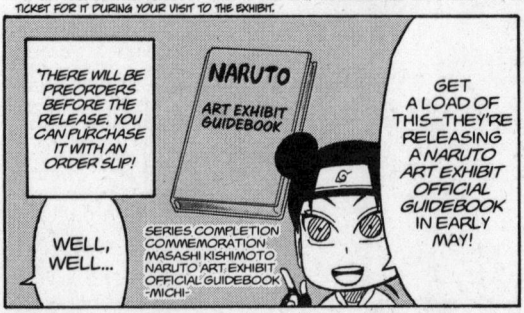

*FOR SALE ONLY AT THE EXHIBIT.
*PREORDERS SHIPPING WITHIN JAPAN ONLY.

*MINI MANGA 1 AND 2 HAVE BEEN INCLUDED AS THEY WERE ORIGINALLY PRINTED IN MAGAZINES IN JAPAN.

MINI MANGA 3:
ROCK LEE'S YOUTH AT FULL POWER COOKING
PART 1: FRENCH TRAINING ARC

ROARR
TWO YEARS LATER...
KONOHA RESTAURANT
OUI!!
BOOSH
ROARR
IT'S THE TASTE OF FRANCE, MY HOME...
YOU'RE NOT FROM FRANCE!!
THIS IS IT! THIS TASTE...
DRIBBLE
THIS IS THE FRUIT OF MY TWO YEARS OF EFFORT!!
BA
I'VE DONE IT, MASTER GUY...
M
WHAT THE HECK?! WHAT DID YOU GO OFF TO TRAIN IN FRANCE FOR?!
OUI!
WAIT, YOU MADE IT?!
THUMBS UP
CHECK OUT THE WORLD OF NARUTO TWO YEARS AFTER THE MANGA, IN THEATERS!!
WHAT'S EVEN HAPPENING HERE?! YOU'RE ALL IDIOTS!!
MHM, MHM.
GWSH
OUIII !!!

THE END

MINI MANGA 4: ROCK LEE'S YOUTH AT FULL POWER COOKING PART 2: NARUTO VS. NEJI ARC

LA TOU...? I THINK YOU'RE MAKING THAT UP, BUT IT SOUNDS LEGIT!!
WELL, NARUTO? CAN YOU SURPASS THIS?
IT'S DONE!! A MIRACULOUS COMBINATION OF FRENCH CUISINE AND RAMEN... LA TOUNI PARA RAMEN!!
YOU'VE GOT TO BE KIDDING ME!!
GAAH
IT'S DONE !!
...
GLUG
GLUG GLU
RAMEN
?!!
HAPPY TO SERVE!
CUT THAT OUT!!
THE WINNER IS... UZUMAKI NARUTO!!
FOR DISHES LIKE RAMEN, IT ACTUALLY TASTES BETTER WITHOUT A TWIST...
SLURP
A STORY OF LOVE CONNECTED TO NARUTO'S FINAL CHAPTER!! CHECK OUT THE LAST: NARUTO THE MOVIE IN THEATERS!!
W-WHAT ARE YOU TALKING ABOUT?!
OR UNCLE WILL GET MAD.
NARUTO... YOU'D BETTER FEED YOUR FUTURE KIDS REAL FOOD...

THE END

MINI MANGA 5: SASUKE VS. THE FOREIGNER!!

...
WHAT ARE... ...YOU ASKING?
OKAY, THEN I'LL COMMUNICATE THROUGH GESTURES.
SHP SHP SHP
...
... WANT?
... YOU ...
WHAT ...
AHH ...
SHPSHPSHP SHP
D... DO NOT MOCK THE UCHIHA-AA!!!
NONE OF IT GOT ACROSS TO HIM!!
BUT HIS PASSION DID GET ACROSS.
GAAAH
<J-JAPANESE NINJA!!>
...
3HEENE
3HEENE
WELL? THAT HAD TO GET IT ACROSS TO YOU...

MINI-MANGA 6: SASUKE VS. THE DENTIST!!

WHRR
REMEMBER...
HUFF
HUFF
THIS IS NOTHING COMPARED TO THE PAIN I'VE EXPERIENCED SO FAR..
HUH? THAT WAS FAST!!!
WHRR
WHAP
I HAVEN'T EVEN STARTED YET!!
G... GUAR-RRGH !!!
VREEEE
DARN YOUUU!
SO IT MAKES NO DIFFERENCE WHETHER I RAISE MY HAND OR NOT?!
THE PAIN OF DENTAL CARE ONLY MAKES YOU STRONGER..
THIS WILL ONLY TAKE A MINUTE.

MINI MANGA 7: SASUKE VS. THE COLORED TILES!!

THA
CK
WHOO
SH
HA!

LEAP
I CAN REACH IT LIKE THIS!!
TAP

SKIIID!
HE WIPED OUT!!
GUARRRGH!!

UH, NO, THAT ONE'S ONLY COLORED WITH YOUR BLOOD!!
UHHHHH
OOZE
HEH HEH HEH.. LOOK. I LANDED ON A COLORED TILE!!
HUFF
HUFF
SASUKE WILL BATTLE ON!!

THE END

BONUS MANGA: MARADA VS. THE LINE!!

WHIRL
!
A LITTLE LONGER AND MY OBJECTIVE WILL BE COMPLETE...
FIDGET
A LITTLE LONGER...
FIDGET
BA
M
I HATE IT WHEN PEOPLE STAND BEHIND ME!!
THERE'S A LINE BEHIND ME TOO?!
I'LL TAKE THIS FAN, AND...
DOOM
SWI
IF IT HAS COME TO THIS...
NG
WHAT DOES THAT FELLA THINK HE'S DOIN'?!
ICHIRAKU
BUHBA
M
END OF THE LINE!
DO THIS!

BONUS MANGA: GROWN-UP SASUKE VS. THE GAP!!

WHEEEEN
SKUF
THE FORCE OF A RASEN-GAN FROM BEHIND'LL PUSH HIM OUT!
IF HE'S STUCK ...
PO——P
WHRRRL
RASENGAN!!
TIME OUT! TIME OUT, BORUTO-OO!!!
SEE YOU IN BORUTO SAIKYO DASH GENER-ATIONS!
I TOTALLY GOT YOU OUT!
NAILED IT!
BA——M
WITHER
WITHER

THE END

You're Reading the WRONG WAY!

NARUTO: CHIBI SASUKE'S SHARINGAN LEGEND reads from right to left, starting in the upper-right corner. Japanese is read from right to left, meaning that action, sound effects and word-balloon order are completely reversed from English order.

HALF HOLLOW HILLS
COMMUNITY LIBRARY
55 Vanderbilt Parkway
Dix Hills, NY 11746